Journey with Grace

A Journey with Grace; A Voice for God

Theresa D. Hammonds

Journey with Grace

Published by
Kingdom Kaught Publishing, LLC
1242 Painted Fern Rd
Denton, Maryland 21629

Copyright © 2015 by Theresa D. Hammonds

All rights reserved.

No part of this book may be reproduced, stored in a retrieval system or transmitted in any form or by any means without written permission of the author.

Published by Kingdom Kaught Publishing, LLC

ISBN 978-0-9824550-9-8

Dedication

I dedicate first and foremost this second volume of Journey with Grace, to the glory of the Almighty God. For without Him this book would not be at all possible. I am His David and Solomon. He has given me the divine gift and purpose of speaking words of wisdom in poetic form.

This gift I have been given by the Almighty, is not only primarily inspired by the Holy Spirit, but God has surrounded me with people in my life that encourage and edify me daily. These people are examples of endurance, strength, joy, wisdom and endless courage. They show and prove that Faith is real for those who believe and trust in the Lord. This dedication is for all the strong women of God that have been there for me over the years. I thank you for your prayers, tolerance, understanding, correction, friendship, concern, support, encouragement, example, wisdom, forgiveness, mercy and inspiration, that has been a driving force for Journey with Grace Volume II. To God be the glory. I therefore acknowledge, Marian Sullins, my natural mother, Johanna Williams, Gina Bartee, Pastor Barbara Palmer, my spiritual mother, Stacy Gardner, Charlene Hawkins, Jamie Massey, Tusajigwe Zawadi Smith, Stephanie Holloman, Armintie Hammonds, Akhirah Padilla, Dana Carcamo, Janeen Freeney, Arnetha Bowens, Avis McElroy, Charmaine Gordon, Sonya Mack and Deloris Shifflett. Any other strong women of God, in my life, reading this dedication page and you have given me any words of encouragement over the years, I thank you as well.

Personal Acknowledgement

Finally, I would like to give a personal dedication to my Bishop, Antonio Palmer and my First Lady, Pastor Barbara Palmer. Being a part of your vision from God is a privilege. Your leadership and Love for God is impeccable and contagious. Thank you for your support over the years. You truly Love God, Love People and Fulfill Needs. Bishop your love for Missions shows the depths of your love for God and people, you are an inspiration to many - who watch. Pastor Barbara, your silent strength and support to the body of Christ is to be admired by many - who watch.

Table of Contents

Introduction i
Vision 1
Disbelief Will Control Your Destiny 3
The Reverence of God 5
The Devil Wants to Rob, Not Kill 7
The Power of Yesterday 9
I Give Myself Away 11
A Mother 13
God Keep Me 15
One Day of Favor 17
Weep 18
Two or Three in My Name 20
Application is the Cure 22
Pray At All Times 23
TEN PERCENT 25
The Model of Christ 27
The Secret Place 29
F. B. I. 31
Seek the Lord 34
Blessed to be a Blessing 36
Debt 38
Do Not Get Tired 40

My Spoils 41
You Know Me Not 43
Reality 45
If You Really Believe 47
The Eyes of the Lord 49
Your Storm 51
Hurt for Hurting Me 54
SNATCHER 56
Thy Excellent Name 58
Death Greets All 60
The Tear 61
The Heart Beat of God 63
In the Wilderness God is Glorified 65
Worship, Witness and Testify 67
Fear Drains, Faith Builds 69
God Seeker 71
The Enemy 73
Endurance 75
The Jacob Change 77
God Wants Givers 79
Stony Heart 81
Provider 83
Exposure 85
Are You a Fisher of Men? 87
Seeker Friendly Church 89

Wisely and Dearly	91
The Test	93
Left Behind	97
The Stripper	99
He is Perfect	101
I. C. U.	103
Citizens of Heaven	106
Armor of God	110
The Land of No Return	112
The Puppet	115
Obedience	118
Glory	122
If You Could See What I See	126
The Passover	130
Hurt People Hurt People	133
The Majority	136
God Encounter	138
Panners	140

Introduction

The Holy Spirit speaks again! Journey with Grace Vol. II will have you captivated from beginning to end. As you travel with Ms. Hammonds again, she will not only reveal to you what the Holy Spirit has to say, but will take you on a much deeper voyage into God's Kingdom. As you read each poem, you will be healed, restored, delivered, rededicated, renewed and possibly led to salvation. Each poem ends with a date and time that the Holy Spirit spoke the words to her, so that when you read each poem, you will be awakened by its authenticity.

I am just a vessel being used by God, a voice that speaks the word, in poetic form. I am a plate of Psalms and Proverbs with a cup of Solomon's wisdom poured on top. I pray for instant healings, restoration and deliverances as you read this book. I pray for joy and peace as you read this book. I hope this book increases your faith and allows you to give more mercy and grace when needed, as it has been given to you. I pray for souls to be saved by reading this book. So sit back, get a cup of coffee or tea and let's begin your journey with grace into God's Kingdom. Enjoy and to God be the glory!

Vision

If you have a vision, you see something bigger than you.
It is a dream, a thought, a plan that has not been
brought into human view.

For a vision always appears like something
that is impossible to do.
How to begin and where to start,
you haven't got a clue.

Living out your vision will take a lot of faith.
Moving forward without knowing,
you must believe is not a waste.

You see God is the giver of vision
because it is bigger than you.
He knew, to you, it would seem impossible.
He knew you wouldn't know what to do.

So to the visionary who calls on God
to find out just what to do,
Know that He will guide your every step,
He will bring clarity into great view.

For a vision is a gift from God,
and your job is to manifest His sight.
Because it is bigger than you,
you will need Him to complete it right.

So if you wake up in the middle of the night with a vision
that is bigger than you,
A thought or dream that seems impossible
and you have no idea what to do.
A vision that seems so unreal,
That even when telling your closest friend
you feel like a fool.

Call on God and ask Him exactly
what He would like you to do.
He'll break it down in small pieces
And it will no longer seem like a monster to you.

For the thoughts and plans He has for you
are greater than you will ever know.
So have faith in Him
and move forward without knowing,
Allow His great power
to finally show.

From God
Through Theresa
6/1/09 - 7:38 P.M.

Disbelief Will Control Your Destiny

If you do not believe you are strong,
but believe you are weak,
then
weak you shall be.

If you do not believe you can become rich,
but believe you are poor,
then
others will always have more.

If you do not believe in yourself,
but believe in what others say,
then
eventually you will behave just that way.

If you do not believe that you can be healed,
but believe you will never be well,
then
you will constantly live in a mental state of hell.

If you do not believe you deserve joy,
but believe you should stay
miserable and depressed,
then your true inner feelings
you will surely suppress.

If you do not believe that the Almighty God controls your destiny,
but believe only you know
what your plans on this earth are truly meant to be,
then the chances are,
only a very small part of your purpose,
if any at all, will He allow you to see.

Do not let disbelief control your destiny!

From God
Through Theresa
5/31/09 - 12:45 P.M.

The Reverence of God

Whether it be for punishment or to show unfailing love,
He is the Almighty, Powerful, Ruler above.

Do you have reverence for God?

He is so powerful that He uses the thunder to speak;
It is so glorious, we all become still, frail and weak.

Do you have reverence for God?

He is so wonderful that He can cast lightning in any direction;
With this awesome flash of light,
there is no need for the sun's reflection.

Do you have reverence for God?

When He is angry He commands storms to suddenly appear;
a true and mighty sign that His presence is here.

Do you have reverence for God?

He keeps the snow, the hail, and the rain in storehouses
until He is ready for their release;
But the minute He sends one of them down in great abundance
the world and animals must cease.

Do you have reverence for God?

He is the creator and maker of all the waters, oceans and seas;
But with one blow from His breath, He can instantly freeze these.

Do you have reverence for God?

The sun is so powerful, when it is in full view;
but yet just a very small accomplishment
of what our God can do.

Do you have reverence for God?

He loads the clouds with moisture,
and then shouts at them to rain;
Sometimes it is used to destroy a place,
Sometimes it is used for earthly gain.

Do you have reverence for God?

We cannot imagine the power of the Almighty;
but even though He is just and righteous,
He does not destroy us.
No wonder people everywhere fear Him,
All who are wise show Him reverence. (Job 37:23-24)

Do you have reverence for God? Do you have reverence for Jesus?

From God
Through Theresa
6/6/09 - 1:11 P.M.

The Devil Wants to Rob, Not Kill

Calling All Soldiers! Calling All Soldiers!

God's angels begin to shout!

We have a battle to fight with Satan
We have to put him out!
The devil wants to rob us, not kill us
don't you see?

If he can strip us of all we have
we might as well be dead,
because we will not be free!

Saints beware of Satan's trap,
he wants to suck us dry.
he wants us to lose all our hope
he wants our faith to die!

he wants to rob us of our joy, our happiness and our peace.
he wants our peaceful nights of sleep,
to instantly cease.

he wants to suck out our gifts, our strength and our praise.
he wants us to stop being obedient to You
and to start doing things his way.

he wants to suck on our anointing, our wisdom and our breath,
he wants to plant seeds of confusion and implant
internal death.
Calling All Soldiers! Calling All Soldiers!
God's angels begin to shout!
We have a battle to fight with Satan
we have to put him out!

From God
Through Theresa
5/31/2009 - 12:38 A.M.

The Power of Yesterday

If you can speak of yesterdays,
what a blessing you have received.
For in a yesterday
was granted life;
no longer just a thought conceived.

You see, to be living in the present
is God's glory at its best.
Because to be living in the now,
means you are passing, enduring or encountering
another test.

For tomorrow is never promised,
and only God knows what your tomorrow will be.
The now is very important
please, just listen to me!

Do not put off today
what you think you can do tomorrow.
For it's like going to the bank
to receive a loan,
You become a very fortunate borrower.

If your tomorrow is given,
then another gracious loan for you.
There is a purpose for your living,
there is something on earth that God
still desires for you, to do.

How fortunate you are
if your once Now, is yesterday.
and what you conceived for tomorrow
God has allowed
to happen just that way.

For Yesterdays are your pasts,
The Present is your now,
The Tomorrows, if answered,
Prove
that everything which happens
is based solely on what the
Almighty allows.

From God
Through Theresa
5/2009 - 9:30 A.M.

I Give Myself Away

In order for you to be seen, oh Lord,
I give myself away.

I crucify myself with You,
Your will, I will obey.

I will no longer live by the flesh
But by The Spirit and in Truth;
In the hope that all will see You in me
And say "It must be the Son of God they sleuth!"

To die to self in order to receive life
is not an easy thing to do.
But to live without God, is death itself;
It is the only way to be renewed.

Because God loved you so much
He sacrificed His only begotten Son.
He had to crucify Him
in order for
your battle to be won.

The battle of living in sin
with no hope of redemption.
The doors of forgiveness being opened wide
with His instant act of ascension.

So in order for you to be seen, Oh Lord,
I give myself away.

I crucify myself with You,
Your will, I will obey.

From God
Through Theresa
5/2009 - 7:15 P.M.

A Mother

This powerful rib taken from man
was a very important part of
God's Master Plan.

For God knew before 'in the beginning'
He would need believers,
So He decided after creating the earth
that woman would be the sole conceiver.

She would be that special vessel
to help Him multiply man.
She was made to be more on earth
than just a helping hand.

Because she has the ordained ability
to manifest you in her womb,
The moment you receive the breath of life,
Her world you would consume.

She would give her life and die for you,
provide you with food, clothing and cover.
Her love is unique and very rare,
This masterpiece is
Called your
"Mother".

She is not an ordinary woman,
for there are many of those around.
She will have qualities like no one else.
Her presence is profound.
You see, to have a "Mother"
is a very special thing.
An abundance of love, joy, peace and security,
are just a few of the things
she will bring.

So make special time
to acknowledge this person called
your "Mother".
Whether you write her, call her,
or go to her grave,
remember her love is like no other.

For just the simple fact that you are here,
will always make her someone
who is very dear.

From God
Through Theresa
4/28/2009 - 2:16 P.M.

God Keep Me

God keep me, for I need to be kept.

I need to be continuously preserved, retained
and observed by You.
No other person or overseer will do.

For Greater is He who is in me, then he that is in the world.
God keep me, for I need to be kept.

The walk of life is hard you see
and cannot be done alone.
There will be many times when you fall to your knees
and when you will need guidance
from the throne.

For Greater is He who is in me, then he who is in the world.
God keep me, for I need to be kept.

There will be times when you are not strong
and your body will be very weak;
These are the times you should depend only on God
and His power will begin to speak.

For Greater is He who is in me, then he who is in the world.
God keep me, for I need to be kept.

You could be that person in debt
and your bills cannot be paid.
No one to call on to help you out,
only God can be your aid.

For greater is He who is in me, then he that is in the world.
God keep me, for I need to be kept.

So without His keeping, you would not be kept,
your life would be a mess.
You have the ultimate watchman
so consider yourself
well blessed.

From God
Through Theresa
5/10/09 - 3:59 P.M.

One Day of Favor

One minute you can be poor,
the next minute you can be rich.
It only takes a second
for your life to suddenly switch.

One minute you can be sick,
the next minute you can be well.
It only takes a second
to be relieved
from a tormenting hell.

One minute you can be alone,
the next minute you can have a friend.
It only takes a second
for your loneliness to end.

One minute you can be unimportant,
the next minute you can be great.
It only takes second
to instantly change your fate.

You see, one day of God's favor is all you need.
One day of favor is a powerful seed.

From God
Through Theresa
6/2009

Weep

Stop all the pretending!
Cease the lies and stop the pain!
Lose all your pride and let
humbleness reign!

For when you are tired,
of being sick and tired
and the pain inside is so deep,
Fall to your knees and do not speak
just allow yourself to Weep.

For God wants to hear the cry of a weeping heart;
To Him it means that it's Him you need.
And if you believe in His Son Jesus,
He will answer your humble plea.

Weeping is a powerful thing
and should be respected
when being used,
for it is an urgent call to God
that we've allowed our souls to be abused.

Let loose of all your pride
and let go of all your pain.
Give your problems, worries
and sorrows to God
and let humbleness reign.

For when you are truly tired,
of being sick and tired
and the pain inside is so deep;
Fall to your knees and do not speak;
just allow yourself to Weep.

For God wants to hear the cry of
a humble and weeping heart.
To Him it means that it's Him you need.
And if you believe in His Son Jesus,
He will answer your dying plea.
And then when you have done, all you can do,
just stand!

From God
Through Theresa
5/31/2009 - 12:40 P.M.

Two or Three in My Name

I do not need a lot of believers
to get done, in the Kingdom,
what needs to be done.

I only need two or three in agreement
for My victories to be won.

For what good
is a large group of believers,
who want to do things their way?
And because they are not in agreement,
My Holy Words go astray.

You see out of a world full of people,
I could have used thousands to spread
My Word.
But instead I chose only twelve disciples,
and taught them what needed to be heard.

For power is not in quantity,
but in the quality
of what is being said.
It only takes two or three in agreement
for My message
to be spread.

Our God is all powerful and can accomplish any
act or task on His own.
But two or three in agreement,
Edifies, Magnifies, and Glorifies Him on the throne.

From God
Through Theresa
6/7/09 - 12:38 P.M.

Application is the Cure

If you know, but do not do
what good is that for me or you?

Knowledge is the key to many things.
It will help you solve the many problems
that life can bring.

So use what you learn,
it will help you to endure.
Application of knowledge is the real cure.

Just to read and to know, The Word,
and not put it to test,
by knowing and not doing
God cannot give you His best.

So do not waste what you know,
It can make your life more secure.
Application of knowledge
is a definite cure.

From God
Through Theresa
6/7/2009 - 12:01 P.M.

Pray At All Times

The man who truly has a relationship with God
but stops praying,
is subjecting himself to sin.

Without regular conversations with God,
the devil can creep within.

How ironic, that the man,
who constantly chooses to live his life doing wrong.

The one who always seems as though,
God grants them to live life exceptionally long.

The one who lives in total self-condemnation
and always wants to do things his way.

The person who refuses to listen and is always reluctant to obey,
is probably the person who is more apt
to constantly pray.

Why would the good man stop praying
while the bad man prays?
Wouldn't you think that it would be the opposite way?

Does the one man think
that he is now too good to fall back into sin?
That with all the world's daily temptations,
the devil cannot creep back in?

While the other man
realizes early, that the only reason
his wrongs have not been discovered,
is because of his constant prayers,
his actions have been covered.

So pray at all times,
in every season, for every reason.

Pray at all times,
whether you are good or you are bad.

Pray at all times,
it is the wisest thing to do.

Praying,
It is the most powerful tool given to man
to help him live life through.

From God
Through Theresa
4/11/2009 - 12:41 P.M.

TEN PERCENT

Ten percent is all God commands,
in order for Him to give you back
one hundred percent.

What a great return on life,
your money is well spent.

For everything you have in life,
it is not even yours to take.
But because you are a child of His,
the riches in His Kingdom
you have been granted to partake.

Why let your fears or selfish ways
stop you from giving what you are told.
You are putting a curse upon yourself,
your promised blessings cannot unfold.

By giving Him your ten percent,
it shows The Almighty, you have great trust.
Now sit and watch with great expectancy,
His promises are a must.

So release your ten percent cheerfully,
as though it were a friend.
He will multiply your giving,
your sacrifice will transcend.

Bring all the tithes into the storehouse
so there will be enough food in my temple.
"If you do" says the LORD of Heaven's Armies,
"I will open the windows of heavens for you."
"I will pour out a blessing so great
you won't have enough room to take it in!"

"Try it!"
"Put Me to the test!" (Malachi 3:10, NLT)
Pressed down, shaken and running over
are the types of blessings He has in store for you.
So release your ten percent cheerfully,
that is all you have to do!

From God
Through Theresa
6/3/2009 - 6:22 P.M.

The Model of Christ

I have been called to be a model of Christ.
Therefore, when you see me,
you should see the reflection of His awesome light.

A light which is gentle and quiet
and comes from deep within;
a light whose beauty is not outward,
and one that is convicted easily by blatant sin.

As Jesus walked this earth,
He was threatened, insulted and beaten.
He carried our sins, in His body, on the cross,
so that our lives would be instantly sweetened.

When I have feelings of hatred,
anger, bitterness or revenge,
I give those feelings instantly to God,
and allow the Holy Spirit to come in.

For our Sovereign God
represents Love, Joy, Patience and Peace.
Therefore,
those types of emotions must quickly be released.

He is my example
and my steps should be the true
reflection of His word.
My actions should be the model,
no need for me to be heard.

For what good are abundant words and great knowledge,
If my actions on earth do not match,
I must strive to be His model; I must show that we are attached.

I have been called to be a model of Christ,
and this task cannot be done on my own.
Therefore, I will always seek the guidance from
The Son
who sits next to Our Father on the Throne.

From God
Through Theresa
7/11/2009 - 3:59 P.M.

The Secret Place

From the outer court to the inner court
is where I long to be.
Removing the veil to that secret place,
The Holy of Holies.

A place where no common man was allowed to enter,
only the high priest.
A sacred place where once a year
man's atonement could be released.

Because of Jesus' sacrifice on the cross,
The Almighty's Glory can now be shown.
Because Jerusalem's veil was ripped,
We can boldly access
His throne.

From the outer court to the inner court,
is where I long to be.
Removing the veil to that secret place,
The Holy of Holies.

So now the dwelling place of our God is exposed,
and access to His Glorious presence
should be feared.

Oh how precious, how Holy, that secret place.
The Holy of Holies,
should always be revered.

From God
Through Theresa
7/13/2009 - 11:20 P.M.

F. B. I.

Faith **B**uilds **I**ntegrity!

God says read My Word and put it to the test.
Dear friends, do not believe every spirit,
but test the spirits to see whether they are from God,
because many false prophets have gone out into the world.
(1 John 4:1)

Investigate Me

Faith Builds Integrity; Integrity Builds Faith.
Believing in the unknown
and having faith in things you cannot see;
trusting when there is no answer
and not knowing what will be.

Investigate Me

Faith Builds Integrity; Integrity Builds Faith.
Test Me!
Put My Words to action
and see if I Am real.
Test the Holy Spirit and see what He reveals.

Investigate Me

Faith Builds Integrity; Integrity Builds Faith.
Faith is believing in things you cannot see,
that is when I can show you
what is really in Me.

I will show you miracles that no one else can do.
They will increase your integrity,
They will build my relationship with you.

Investigate Me

Faith Builds Integrity; Integrity Builds Faith.
I dare you to find that secret place
that will bring you to your knees.
For access has been granted to all
The Holy of Holies.

For even if your faith is
as small as a mustard seed,
you will be able to SPEAK a mulberry tree
into the deep blue sea.

Investigate Me

Faith Builds Integrity; Integrity Builds Faith.
Faith opens the door of undeserved grace
from the Almighty God above.
Through Jesus Christ we have been justified
and therefore, can share His Glory
and receive His abundant love.

But first, in order for anyone to have this type of relationship with Me,

Investigate Me!

Faith Builds Integrity; Integrity Builds Faith.

From God
Through Theresa
7/17/2009 - 12:12 P.M.

Seek the Lord

Seek the Lord!
Chase Him!
Follow Him day and night.

Take Him with you
when you are doing wrong.
Take Him with you
when you are living right.

Search for Him, look for Him,
like you have just lost your child.
A search that just won't quit,
one that will last a very long while.

Wake up in the midnight hour
with thoughts of Him racing in your mind.
Thoughts of Him racing so intensely,
you leave all other worries behind.

Look for Him, like you looked for love.
A search that did not quit,
until it was found.
And then when you found your true love,
no one else was needed around.

Seek the Lord!

Chase Him!

Chase Him like there is no tomorrow.
I guarantee, if you put Him first,
He will give you abundant peace and remove your sorrow.

Do you seek the Lord?
Do you look for Him, like you have lost your mother in the store?
Does your heart ache when you cannot find Him?
That type of love that cannot be ignored.

Seeking the Lord should never stop.
It is something daily you must do.
For He is the ultimate Savior
and His blood was shed for me and for you.

Seek the Lord!

Chase Him!

Follow Him day and night.

Take Him with you
when you are doing wrong.
Take Him with you
when you are living right.

From God
Through Theresa
7/26/2009 - 7:21 A.M.

Blessed to be a Blessing

Today I am blessed, because I'm awake.
I have been given another chance
of this life to partake.

I am blessed to open my eyes
and look all around,
to view God's creations and hear all the sounds.

I am blessed to have work during the day
and I am able to prioritize my own plans.
To walk with both my feet and to
use both of my hands.

I am blessed to be a blessing

I am blessed to have sufficient food to eat.
I could be homeless, living on the cold lonely streets.

I am so fortunate to have clothes on my back;
There really is not much that I truly lack.

I am blessed to be a blessing

I am blessed that I am not sick.
That all of my illnesses come and go
very quick.

That my health is good and my mind is well.
That in this body of mine
Satan cannot dwell.

I am blessed to be a blessing

I am blessed to be comfortable and not to be poor.
For money can definitely make your life
more secure.

I am blessed to be a blessing

I am blessed to give and not to take.
All my selfish ways I must quickly break.

I am blessed to be a blessing

I was lost, but now I am found
God has turned my whole life around.

I am blessed to be a blessing.

From God
Through Theresa
7/31/2009 - 10:59 P.M.

Debt

The devil wants you to spend your money on worthless things
because he knows once you have them
all the headaches and problems they will bring.

At first it will seem great and you will be very content.
But then when the struggle begins,
You will have feelings of remorse and resent.

Believers, we must learn the difference between wants and needs.
Once we learn the difference, God will allow us
to succeed.

For when we master a little, He will give us much more.
He will open Heaven's window
and blessings will begin to pour.

If we spend our money more freely in the world
than we do in the church,
we give Satan permission
to begin his wicked search.

A search for believers who spend their money
on worldly distractions.
The Devil wants to Encourage
the Believers Transactions!

If the devil can encourage
the way you spend,
there will be nothing left
for the Kingdom to transcend.

What you will have left to spend
will be so small
that you will be afraid to give God your all.

The devil would love for all God's children
to be in great DEBT,
then the Church, God's Kingdom, will no longer be
his greatest threat.

From God
Through Theresa
8/2/2009 - 5:42 P.M.

Do Not Get Tired

Do not get tired
even though the fight may seem long.

Do not get tired
even though everything around you is going wrong.

Do not get tired
even though others say you should quit.
Do not allow their words of negativity to transmit.

Do not get tired
even though all your friends may leave

Do not get tired
but just continue to believe.
For just when you get tired, your victory is near
and all of God's blessings will soon begin to appear.

Do not get tired,
fight all your battles to the very end.
God already has the victory,
we just have to contend.

From God
Through Theresa
8/9/2009 - 12:20 P.M.

My Spoils

Will you be on the frontline for God
when the spoils are given out?

Will you be able to take back what was yours,
with a bold and mighty shout?

Will you have so much to give
that there will be an overflow?

Will you share graciously,
even with those who did not sow?

The enemy has taken your things
and you have to take them back.
When God wants to release your spoils
you must be ready to attack!

For in the spoils will be the answers to a lot of your prayers.
Clarity will be in abundance,
and you will forget all of your worries and your cares.

God is the Master, Who opens and closes
each and every door.
Will you be in position
when His blessings begin to pour?

Will you be on the frontline for God,
when the spoils are given out?!
Will you be able to take back what was yours,
with a bold and mighty shout?!

From God
Through Theresa
8/9/2009 - 3:48 P.M.

You Know Me Not

You think you know me, but you know me not.
For what you see is but a dot.

If I ask you now, the color of my eyes
could you answer with just one try?

Have you listened to the things I've said?
or have they gone straight through your head?

A clown with a sad face,
Happy and sad in the same place.

The sky is blue, the sun is bright,
does that mean the weather is right?
There could be rain. There could be hail.
Only God knows what will prevail.

When babies cry, do you know why?
Are they wet? Are they dry?
Are they happy? Are they sad?
Are they hungry or just plain mad?

A clown with a sad face,
Happy and sad in the same place.
You look at me, you see a smile
but we must sit and talk a while.

For my smile could be hiding a lot of pain,
but to share with all, what would I gain?

Some people are not worthy of one's
deepest thoughts, it becomes a tool
to destroy their heart.

A clown with a sad face,
Happy and sad in the same place.

Sometimes what you see isn't always there.
Sometimes what we get, isn't always fair.

A clown with a sad face,
Happy and sad in the same place.

From God
Through Theresa
1999

Reality

Reality
The sum of all that is real, absolute and unchangeable.

Reality
All things possessing existence or essence in its totality.

At what time does one receive the gift of reality?
At birth, at home, or near their senility?

If we are told that black is evil and white is pure,
that the rich really care for the welfare of the poor,
then what is reality?

Is a poor man's reality the same as the rich?
Or does the environment he lives in, make
his reality switch?

If we are told something is true, right from the start,
then is my reality wrong, if what I now
believe in, is truly in my heart?

Ones' reality, ones' mentality
are they one in the same?
What is real and what we think,
which one do we claim?

Reality
The choice between falsehoods and that which is real.
Why do we choose the first and not the last?
Are falsehoods easier to conceal?

Reality
Satan or Christianity
The power of God's real Word or the devil's words, which aid to your insanity.

If your mentality is fake and your reality is real,
then your true inner soul is being concealed.

What people see, is not what they get,
and you surely are losing your
greatest gift yet
Your own Reality!

From God
Through Theresa
10/14/1997

If You Really Believe

If you really believe
that God is truly in control,
then step back and allow
Him to take His righteous role!

A role that is in control of everything
that happens to you.
All you need to do is sit back,
listen, endure, and see it through.

When you try to take control,
it shows that you lack trust.
Then when things do not go your way,
you feel it was unjust.

So if you really believe
that God is in complete control,
then whether the outcome is good or bad
you will not allow it to affect your soul.

For God loves the cry of a humble heart,
because then He can step in,
and if you allow Him to do His job,
you will end up the victor and surely win.

If you really believe
that God is in control,
then you will always have abundant peace.
You will realize the final outcome is His Will
and your madness will instantly cease.

So stop trying to play God,
It is impossible for you to do.
You will never have all the answers,
It was a job not meant for you.

From God
Through Theresa
8/15/2009 - 12:30 P.M.

The Eyes of the Lord

God is looking for a "particular" kind of person;
a person that will allow Him to show Himself strong.
A person whose desire is to live their life holy
and not live their life intentionally doing wrong.

God is looking for a Saint that is aggressive and proactive.
God is searching for a vessel,
where He can become active.
God is looking for a person who is truly divine.
He is searching for a dwelling place
that He can call "Mine".

God's eyes are looking for a person,
who truly has His heart.
A person who loves Him so dearly
that you will not be able
to tell them apart.

God is not just looking for the person that is
so called, "Saved".
His eyes will be monitoring closely,
all of your daily actions
and how you really behave.

God's eyes are searching desperately,
for the person that is chasing Him.
A heart that is opened so graciously,
that He can immediately come in.

The eyes of the Lord
are searching the earth
for a person with a "particular" kind of behavior.
Not just a person who believes in The Word,
but a person He can support and
release abundant favors.

God is not looking for the normal man,
but a "particular" person you must be.
A person in whom the Holy Spirit can rise
for the whole wide world to see.

From God
Through Theresa
8/17/2009 - 10:40 P.M.

Your Storm

Your storm is in the palm of His hand

Wicked winds of destruction,
darkness of turmoil and despair,
A whirlwind of confusion,
no one there to show they care.

Your storm is in the palm of His hand

Holding you against your will,
forcing your back up against the wall,
wanting you to solve it yourself,
wanting you to fall.

Your storm is in the palm of His hand

Your head hurts and your eyes are red
No thoughts of enduring,
you wish you were dead.

Your storm is in the palm of His hand

You wake up in the morning
and the clouds are still around.
Sleepless nights control your evenings,
your peace cannot be found.

Your storm is in the palm of His hand

God looks down in the palm of His hand and
He sees what you are going through.
He can see your every action
Your whole world is in His view.

Your storm is in the palm of His hand

He only allows to happen
as much as He knows you can bear.
He knows your strengths and weaknesses.
This God, Your God, who made you,
has counted every strand of hair!

Your storm is in the palm of His hand

He waits to see if your faith is strong,
and if you are willing to endure the test.
He wants to see if you trust Him,
instead of giving up and being depressed.

Your storm is in the palm of His hand

He closes His hand tightly,
while your storm is in His fist.
He will not allow anything to happen to you
as long as He is in the midst.

Your storm is in the palm of His hand

When He thinks your storm should be over
and you have endured the test,
He opens the windows of Heaven
and you are suddenly blessed.
His hand is gently opened,
as He allows the light to come right in.
He is so pleased you put all
your trust in Him;
He gives you an awesome grin!

Your world of problems may seem big to you,
but to Him they are very small.
I think it was designed just that way,
so that He could receive a call.

Your Storm is in the palm of His hand

From God
Through Theresa
9/10/2009 - 4:38 P.M.

Hurt for Hurting Me

Do you hurt when you hurt Me?

Does your heart ache when we disagree?
When you want to do wrong and I want you to do right,
does it disturb you when we begin to fight?

I say "Be celibate," but you choose to fornicate,
knowing in your heart that it is much better to wait.

Do you respect your parents, as I have commanded of you?
Do you do all the things that they ask you to do?

Do you feed the homeless, when you have money to give?
Or do you only care about how comfortable you live?

Do you hurt when you hurt Me?

Do you talk about me to your friends?
Or are you more concerned with the earthly trends?

Are you your brother's keeper when they are in need?
Or do you quickly forget your spiritual creed?

Do you always tell the truth instead of lies?
When you know it is something I truly despise?

Do you hurt when you hurt Me?

Do you worship other types of gods?
Knowing very well they are all facades?

Do you give me My ten percent?
Or do you rob from Me with no consent?

Do you hurt when you hurt me?

Do you accept the Lord Jesus as your One and Only Savior?
Or do you choose to live your life in constant sinful behavior?

Do you hurt when you hurt Me?

From God
Through Theresa
8/18/2009 - 10:09 P.M.

SNATCHER

Are you a Snatcher?

Are you willing to pull someone else in trouble
out of their own mess?
Are you willing to forget your own problems?
And become a part of someone else's test?

Are you willing to be someone else's strength?
When clearly, they are just too weak.
Are you willing to devote all of your time?
When they have reached their last peak.

Are you willing to speak life into their heart
when death is knocking at their door?
Will you become their small window of light,
when living in darkness is at its core?

Will you feed them and shelter them
when no one else seems to care?
Will you sacrifice your life and things
and begin to openly share?

Are you a Snatcher for God?
Seeking daily to pull sinners out of their own mess?
Are you concerned about saving souls
and honoring all of God's request?

Are you willing to stay up all night
to intercede on another's part?
Are you willing to forget your flesh
and become a true servant of the heart?

Are you a Snatcher for the Almighty God?
Do you really understand what you must do?

Let God Snatch you!
As you Snatch them!
A victory in great view!

From God
Through Theresa
9/19/2009 - 11:10 A.M.

Thy Excellent Name

God wants everyone to know His excellent name
We were made in God's likeness and a mirror
we must be.
Open your mouth with a perfected praise
and decree to the world God's Glory!

He is the El Shaddai, El Elyon, Elohim
and the great Yahweh!
The Beginning and the End
The Author and Finisher of our faith
The Master of earth always!

He is Jehovah Nissi, Jehovah Jirah
and the great Jehovah Shalom.
He is All knowing, All powerful and All present,
Across the whole earth His spirit roams.

He is the healer, the listener, the confidante
and a true and faithful friend.
He is the One who sacrificed His Son, Jesus, and caused Him
to ascend.

He is the creator of the Heavens and the Earth
and even the Master of Hell.
There is no place thought of
where the Holy One does not dwell.

Lift Him up, for He is worthy and all praises He is due.
Abundant Mercy and undeserved Grace
have been freely given to you.

For He's the Great I Am
So give Him all the glory and all the fame.
Father God, Almighty God
How Excellent is Thy Name!

From God
Through Theresa
11/29/2009 - 4:33 p.m.

Death Greets All

If I know anything, if I know anything at all,
ashes to ashes and dust to dust
death will greet us all

I do not know how many stars are in the sky
or how many different creatures live in the seas
I do not know how many hairs are on my head
or the cures for all human disease

But ashes to ashes and dust to dust is a phrase
that is well known to man
If we all ever agree to one thing,
we know this is in the final plan

For God made man from the earth
and the earth he shall return
He'll either go to Heaven or
to Hell he'll surely burn

If I know anything, if I ever know anything at all,
ashes to ashes and dust to dust
We will all receive that call

From God
Through Theresa
11/29/2009 - 5:14 p.m.

The Tear

Things in your life sometimes have to be torn apart
So God can see where you stand.
If everything in your life were to always
go right, then there would be no
need for God's sovereign hand.

The hand that shows up in the midst of your storm,
when no one else seems to care.
The powerful hand that restores and repairs
and knows just how much you can bear.

You see, to be torn apart can be very painful
and none of us like pain,
But it is a very important process,
needed to receive our personal gain.

God shows His greatest strength
when we are in a broken state.
For that is the time when we fall to our knees
and finally tell the world it has to wait.

Ripped, Torn, Shattered and Abused!
Those are the times when our mighty God
likes to be used.
During those times, He promises to heal
During those times you can make your appeals.

When you are torn apart
your faith gets put to the test
and if you endure, you will be surely blessed.

From God
Through Theresa
1/1/2010 - 9:03 p.m.

The Heart Beat of God

Pacing, Racing,

The Heart Beat of the Almighty God

Pure, clean, always forgiving,
Flowing with abundant love,
The reason for life, the reason for giving

Never missing a beat,
Never having a moments sleep

The Heart Beat of the Almighty God

A beat that penetrates through all of
our souls and stops us from
our own destruction
A beat so powerful and strong
it can become a silent voice with spiritual instructions

A beat so great that flows with such force;
It will wake you in your sleep
and if your relationship is not right with Him
will cause your spirit to weep

The Heart Beat of the Almighty God
The greatest heart beat on earth
The Heart Beat of the Almighty God
Your true heart beat at birth

From God
Through Theresa
1/1/2010 - 9:33 p.m.

In the Wilderness God is Glorified

Oh this desolate and deserted place called Wilderness
A place beyond settlement or permanent stay
That place where you feel lost and left completely astray

The Place where God is glorified

A place of thirst, hunger and deprivations of all sorts
A place where you believe you have no human support

That place where you wander to be tested and tempted
The Place you wish God would label exempted

The place where God is glorified

A place where overcoming the physical and psychological becomes real
A place where all your strengths and weaknesses are revealed
A place to withdraw from the world
to face the reality of oneself and the reality of God
A place with no pretenses or facades

The place where God is glorified

The wilderness, the best place for God
and His shepherds to lead their sheep
A place of great alienation, where God's voice truly speaks

The place where transformation and transition take hold
The place where Jesus Christ is, Behold!

The place where God is glorified

From God
Through Theresa
1/18/2010 - 12:42 p.m.

Worship, Witness and Testify

We worship You in spirit and in truth
We adore You, oh magnificent and powerful God
We are in awe of Your every word
We come before You with a humble and reverent heart,
for You are the Lord of Lords and the King of Kings

Father God, how unworthy are we, to even be in Your presence
For You sacrificed Your only begotten Son, for our sins, that we may come boldly to Your throne and make our supplications known to You

Yahweh, Jehovah
Father full of mercy and abundant grace
We draw near to You, and You will draw near to us (James 4:8)
I must go tell the world about God's power and His Grace
I must tell the world about His love for me, deliverances and His forgiving spirit.
I must "Therefore, go and make disciples of all nations, baptizing them in the name of the Father and of the Son and of the Holy Spirit, and teaching
them to obey everything He commands.
And God will be with me until the very end of the age" (Matthew 28:19, 20).

"You will receive power when the Holy Spirit comes on you, and you will be my witnesses". (Acts 1:8).

"I tell you the miracles themselves. I tell you the truth, anyone who has faith in me will do what I have been doing. He will do even greater things than these, because I am going to the Father" (John 14:12).

"You cannot help speaking about what you have seen and heard" (Acts 4:20).

Therefore Almighty God
Creator of the Heavens and the Earth and the Master of Hell
I testify You are the Lord of Lords and the King of Kings

I testify that you sacrificed Your only begotten Son for my sins
I testify that once I was lost, but now I am found
I testify You have renewed me in the Spirit
and have transformed me

I testify that You have performed many miracles in my life
and will perform many more miracles through me

I testify that You are my strength
I testify that I am nothing without You
I testify that Jesus Christ is Lord!

From God
Through Theresa
1/18/2010 - 2:03 p.m.

Fear Drains, Faith Builds

Fear says stop and Faith says go.
Faith says move forward and Fear says take it slow.

Fear wants to cripple you, when Faith says to walk.
Fear wants you to run, when great opportunities knock.

Fear causes you to want answers, when answers are not there.
Faith says to continue moving, without worries and without cares.

Faith believes in things you cannot see.
Fear is the catapult that causes us to flee.

Faith gives you the power to go on when you want to quit.
Fear tells you to give up, be quiet and to sit.

Fear stops us from saying things that need to be said.
Faith says speak the truth, no need to feel dread.

Fear is the demon that stops us from attaining success.
Faith is the angel that surpasses every test.

Fear is the drainer of all hopes and of all dreams.
It is the master blocker of the most powerful schemes.

But Faith is that powerful thing that can cast out all fear.
Faith is God's love, our strength to persevere.

For God's perfect love cast out all fear (John 4:18)

And that is when God's blessings
and opportunities can really appear.

From God
Through Theresa
6/29/2008 - 10:27 a.m.

God Seeker

I look to the left
I look to the right
I look through the dark,
to search for the light

I look up
I look down,
I search all over this earthly ground

I look above
I look below,
I look for the answers
to things that I do not know

I am a God seeker

When I wake, I want You near
When I cry out, I want You to be the first to hear
When I close my eyes, I want You to lie next to me
When I am in great trouble, I want You to answer my very last plea

I am a God seeker

I want to long and to thirst for Your every Word
So when You speak to me, You will surely be heard

I am a God seeker

Man is not sufficient enough to end such a search
Nor priest, nor pastor, nor any leader of any synagogue or church

I am a God seeker

It will be You that I long for every night and everyday
It is You I desire to worship and to obey

I completely surrender my absolute will unto You,
No other God or idol will do

I am a God seeker

From God
Through Theresa
1/24/2010 - 1:35 p.m.

The Enemy

Oh hostile force who stays awake,
looking for souls to consume and to take

The one who accuses and wants you to carry great guilt,
The one who destroys
after progress is built
Satan, Lucifer or the Father of Lies,
The controller of sin, the master disguise

The Prince of the bottomless pit,
the Angel of the abyss,
The god of the evil world, where only darkness exists

The tempter, the dragon, the serpent, the deceiver,
The ultimate adversary for the true believer
The ruler of demons, the great infidel,
The fallen angel from heaven,
whose home is called " Hell"

So be alert all Saints and protect your mind,
For this is where Satan spends most of his time

Know the enemies voice
and do not permit him to speak,
This is how he sneaks in;
this is how he makes you weak

So resist the devil and he will flee,
Take authority over him
in Jesus' mighty name
and
you will remain free

From God
Through Theresa
1/30/2010 - 11:05 p.m.

Endurance

When you get strength from somewhere,
but you don't know how
"If I can just make it through, this one thing!"
Is your solemn vow

When your eyes are weak and your legs want to give
When your heart is still beating
But you aren't sure you want to live

Endurance

When your mind feels heavy and ready to explode,
but you keep on moving, you carry the load

When you do and care more for others
than you do for yourself
Sacrificing everything,
even compromising your own health

Endurance

Where does this secret strength come
from that creeps in the air?
Where does this type of power come from
in your time of great despair?

A power that surpasses what can be done in the flesh
The only power that turns chaos and stress
into a peaceful mesh.

The Power of the Almighty God

For only He knows - how much you can really bear
You see, this is when God shows how much He truly cares

He steps right in, when you want to stop
He will pick you up
He will not let you drop

Without Him the word Endurance would not exist
It is needed to fight the devil
It is the ultimate power used to resist

<u>ENDURANCE!</u>

IS WHEN

U AND GOD **RUN** TO THE **END**

A true victory
with your powerful friend

From God
Through Theresa
1/31/2010 - 10:00 a.m.

The Jacob Change

When the power of God really touches your heart,
there will be definite signs that set you apart.

The flesh will die and the spirit will rise;
Your friends and your family
will not believe
the change in you
that they see with their eyes.

Now you are sober, once you were a drunk;
You thought drinking was the solution to all of life's junk.
Now you are clean, you used to smoke crack;
Getting high was your answer, when you felt under attack.

Now you are honest, you used to tell lies;
It was the protector of your heart,
your master disguise.
Now you forgive, you used to hold a grudge;
You thought you had the right, to be the final judge.

Now you are abstinent, you used to fornicate;
Loneliness was not an option, it was impossible to wait.
But then the spirit of God really entered your soul;
You let go of death and He began to make you whole.
But by the renewal of your mind you are being transformed;
Doing things in the world, you no longer conform. (Romans12:2)

The Father will be pleased
when He looks down on you;
He will change your name, He will make you brand new.

So when God has a mission
in store for you,
The flesh must die, you have to be renewed.

Just as He changed the names of
Abram, Sarai and a man called Jacob,
Your true acceptance of God
will be your
ultimate make up.

From God
Through Theresa
1/31/2010 - 5:50 p.m.

God Wants Givers

Give Love
For it will restore a broken heart

Give Time
For tomorrow is never promised

Give Care
For it is the best medicine for healing

Give Guidance
For it controls possible mistakes

Give Life
For death tears down and destroys

Give Wisdom
For knowledge is power

Give Money Cheerfully
For you will get it back tenfold

Give Attention
For someone desperately needs to be heard

Give Correction
For chastisement is a true sign of love

Give Praise
For it is your greatest gift to God

Give Worship
For a true friend He will be

Give The Word of God
For it is the key to Salvation

Give yourself to God
For you will see Him in Eternity

When you give, you will always receive
With an open hand, Trust in the Lord
You must believe!

From God
Through Theresa
2/21/2010 - 7:51 a.m.

Stony Heart

Hard and cold,
your feelings for life have died
Bitterness and pain submerge,
there are no longer true emotions inside

Trust is gone and faith is now small
Your eyes are shut
You've created a wall

God please remove my stony heart

Tears no longer fall
Smiles have gone to sleep
Anger takes control
Your heart no longer weeps

God please remove my stony heart

Giving has stopped and taking has begun
Others are no longer first
You've become number one!

God please remove my stony heart

If you let God in
He will soften your heart
He can heal all the wrongs
He can put in view a new start
With God comes forgiveness,
love, joy and great peace
He's an internal cleanser,
a tool for release

He can take your stony heart
and make it as pliable as clay

All your demons will be called out
They will not be allowed to stay!

God can remove your stony heart
Perfection He does not seek
He loves to help the pure in heart
He loves to save the weak

Once the stones have been removed,
restoration can take place
Your heart will be repaired
Your past will be erased

From God
Through Theresa
5/4/2010 - 10:30 a.m.

Provider

All my needs are met
There is nothing that I need

He hears all of my requests
He answers all of my pleas

Jehovah, My Master
Jehovah, My Supplier
Jehovah Jirah
You are the Supreme Provider

I have food on my table
and clothes on my back
I have a roof over my head
There is nothing that I lack

When I go through storms in life
that bring me to my knees,
Some based on bad decisions
and consequences
I do not want the world to see

Jehovah, My Master
Jehovah, My Supplier
Jehovah Nissi
You are the Supreme Provider

You pick me up and wipe my tears
and you quickly set me free
You always love
You never judge
You take good care of me

You never come when I think you should
But never are You late
You always show up when I need you the most,
while man tells me I have to wait

As long as I have You in my life,
being without, will never be
For You fulfill everything I could ever want,
Your Spirit dwells in me

Jehovah, My Master
Jehovah, My Supplier
Jehovah Jirah
You are the Supreme Provider!

From God
Through Theresa
5/4/2010 - 1:27p.m.

Exposure

Stop Hiding!
Remove the Crap!
Finally confess to God,
the things you lack.

Become transparent and
release your sins.
Take the power away from the Devil
and let the Holy Spirit in!

Do not worry
about what the world thinks about you.
It's not important you see.
It will only delay the time,
that you can spend with Thee.

God doesn't care about what you have done,
your salvation means more to Him.
For He is a forgiving God
So expose yourself within!

Your soul will have peace
no more internal fight.
Expose your darkness
let in the light.

Exposure is good
because it allows you to move ahead.
Until that is done, you are alive, but very much dead.

From God
Through Theresa
5/4/2000 - 2:30 p.m.

Are You a Fisher of Men?

Are you willing to go into the deep
where the unknown creatures live low?

Are you willing to go into the darkness
where the light can really show?

To lead and not follow
To be the example you were called to be.
To be such a sign of righteousness
that you can tell the Sinner,
"Follow Me"

Are you a fisher of men?

Are you willing to go out into the wicked waters
and cast out your net to save the lost?
Even if your net breaks,
Are you willing to sacrifice the cost?

Fish roaming aimlessly underneath
without any direction,
seeking for food at the surface
only because of the light's reflection.

Looking for the right bait
that will hook onto their soul.
Being brought to the surface
only to face death,
the only path to leave
the dark and murky hole.

Are you a fisher of men?

Are you willing to go out into the sea
only to catch just one?

Is catching one sincere, hungry fish
better than receiving a ton?

Are you a fisher of men?
Are you a fisherman for Jesus?

From God
Through Theresa
5/15/2010 - 8:00 a.m.

Seeker Friendly Church

Do you attend a church that white-washes God's word.
Preachers preaching the gospel, but not delivering
the message as powerfully as they should?

Instead of leaving convicted
Sinners and Saints depart feeling good.

Giving sermons about all kinds of sins
but making them seem small.
Causing Sinners and Saints to use
God's mercy and forgiveness
as a reason to refuse His call.

Does your repentance
become an easy tool to be released from doing wrong?
Does going to church on Sundays
become an act of kindness to God
as long as the service is not too long?

Do you attend a church that
clearly loves God,
but does not speak the hard and solid truth?
Afraid to lose its' members
so basically the Saints run loose.

Is your Church seeker-friendly
when God wants to save souls?
Sacrificing the true medicine
that has the cure to make them whole.

So speak the truth and
stop sugar coating the Word,
even though it may really hurt.

For that is the only way
true restoration takes place
and God can remove their dirt.

From God
Through Theresa
8:52 a.m. - 5/15/2010

Wisely and Dearly

Should I love You wisely?
or should I love You dearly?

For dearly love is love with a great cost
Loving no matter what it takes
Loving no matter what the loss.

But if I love You wisely
then I am loving You with great judgment
and with basic common sense.

I might think Your decisions
for me are hard at times
I will probably put up a good self-defense.

Loving You dearly means that when I want to
do something that is clearly
not good for me to do
I become more concerned about Your feelings
and rather give in, then to see You blue.

But loving You wisely
means that if You have to correct me
and take the chance that my feelings may become hurt
then it will surely be worth it, especially if the
correction causes a positive convert.

Loving wisely means loving with boundaries and within logical reasons
Loving dearly means loving freely and changing your love depending on the other person's seasons.

Loving dearly is like "loving someone to death"
you'll sacrifice anything for them
until you take your very last breath.

But loving wisely is like "loving someone to live"
you want the very best for them
but you think before you give.

So now that you understand the difference between these
two types of love clearly;
The Almighty, All Powerful Jesus Christ
Is the Only One
Who really knows how to use them fairly.

From God
Through Theresa
8:24 a.m. - 5/21/2010

The Test

Everything in my life was going just fine
Not a single worry was on my mind
And out of nowhere,
when I was feeling my best,
Satan challenged God to put me
Through The Test.

Now the test is a place
where none of us like to go,
A place where Satan tries to take us below.

He gets permission to tempt us
to do things we should not do,
He tries to destroy us
because our spirits have been renewed.

He won't tempt you with situations
that you now have under control,
He will shake areas in your life
that will affect your soul.

So what is your weakness?
And that is where He will be,
The place that He thinks will
once again bring you to your knees.

He wants you to fall down and not to endure
The Test
He wants to show our Father
That He will be the winner of this contest.

He wants to prove that your faith is weak
He wants to destroy your trust in Him
and make us believe our problem is very bleak.

But if you endure the Test
Do not budge, and do not move
Our Mighty Father has made some promises to you.

He said He would never leave you nor forsake you
in times of great need.
He said He likes the humble in heart and will show
His awesome strength
when you fall to your knees.

He said we are the head and not the tail
He said if you put your trust in Him
You would always prevail.

He said we are above and not below
My God said that if I obey, He will set me high above all nations.
His strength will really show.

He said be strong and be of good courage; be not afraid.
With just the power of His voice
the heavens and the earth were instantly made.

Gentiles you were, but adopted into the family of Hebrews
He said I give you power to tread over serpents and scorpions
and nothing will hurt you.

He said my enemies will rise and be smitten before my face.
Seven directions they will flee,
instantly removed, without a trace.

He said when I cry unto Him
my enemies will turn back
My powerful Father will cease their violent attacks.

He said if I cry out to Him and do His will
He will hear me out of his Holy hill.

He said if I cry to Him when I am in trouble
He will deliver me out of my distress.
He will take care of my situation
He will clean up my mess.

He said as a lion, the righteous are bold
He gives us confidence
His magnificent glory we behold.

He said by His Son's stripes
we have been justified and healed
Now we can boldly stand before our Father
Our requests answered
Our sins no longer revealed.

Everything in my life was going just fine
Not a single worry was on my mind
And out of nowhere,
when I was feeling my best
Satan challenged God to put me
Through The Test.

For true servants of the Almighty God
A Test will come and A Test will go
Stand, be strong and take every blow.

For this is just a battle between Satan
and our All-powerful God
He is the one who holds the Sovereign rod.

He wants to see if we trust Him and have undying Faith
He wants to put another victory right
in Satan's face!

From God
Through Theresa
6/24/2010 - 7:27 a.m.

Left Behind

My world suddenly came to a rapid stop
and silence consumed the air.

The sound of my heartbeat grew
louder and louder,
as each beat overtook my ears.

Vivid memories of you flashed before me quickly,
as tears clouded the vision of my eyes.
Your voice enslaved my every thought,
with words of wisdom
and words of correction, your voice of chastisement
I no longer despise.

Even though the sun was shining,
a sadness captured my heart.

Just one more minute, just one more second,
Why did we have to part?

It wasn't time for you to leave me yet,
There were things we still had to do.

I thought I would be prepared for this,
I thought I knew the rules.

Whether a death is expected
or catches you by surprise,
grieving over a lost one,
is never ever kind.

And even though the one who has left the earth,
to be with the Father in eternity
will be more than fine.

I now stand silently by myself
I have been "Left Behind."

From God
Through Theresa
7/27/2010 - 12:06 a.m.

The Stripper

Just when you think you got it just right.
God comes along and takes another bite.

Transforming into His likeness
is not an easy task at all.
Many are chosen, but only a few will receive the call.

This call takes hard work and great discipline.
This call will mandate constant "Stripping"
from within.

When you allow Jesus to use you
and to dwell within
A repetitive cleansing is needed
in order for you and Him to be very close friends.

If it wasn't for His bloodshed, we would never
be free from our own sin.
So this is why the "Stripping" must begin.

If you truly love Him and allow Him,
He will strip you every day.
So it will be very important
to listen to Him
and to hear what He has to say.

As you allow Him, He will begin to speak;
He will bring forth your areas that are
very weak.

The areas in your life that you
have made a mess;
Those areas in your life, you have consistently
failed His tests.

He will begin to strip
them one by one;
This type of stripping is never done.

Because just as you think you got it just right,
Almighty God will come back and take another bite.

Becoming transformed into His likeness is not an
easy task at all,
Especially for those who are serious about
receiving the call.
So if you are the person who really wants
The Holy Spirit to dwell within,
Get ready for a life-long journey and
allow your "Stripping" to begin.

From God
Through Theresa
7/29/2010 - 8:30 p.m.

He is Perfect

His work is ever so wonderful
His mind never changing
His thoughts never a flaw
should leave man breathless
and completely in awe.

He is ever so perfect

No faults, no doubts
No room for improvement
His light penetrates the dark.
No blemishes, No scars
No mistakes at all
His presence leaves a powerful mark.

He is ever so perfect

The Alpha, the Omega
The Beginning and The End
Your only true and consistent friend.

He is ever so perfect

Heaven is His home
The earth is His footstool
and Hell is even His creation.
He controls and owns everything on this earth
He provides escape to all temptations.

He is ever so perfect

There is no shadow of turning for Him
No turning left or turning right
Once life is spoken into the atmosphere
He moves forward in His great delight.

He is ever so perfect
In Him abundant Grace, Mercy,
Forgiveness and Love
abide
Because of the bloodshed of His only begotten Son
Our sins can no longer reside.

He is ever so perfect
He is ever so lovely
He is the Great I Am!

From God
Through Theresa
7/9/2010 - 10:45 a.m.

I. C. U.

The line between
life and death is thin.
Where you will end up is based
on the ruler within.

When you lay there with
your eyes closed tight,
Satan and God will begin their
territorial fight.

The final outcome is always
based on God's supreme will.
While your loved ones wait helplessly,
they have to be still.

As God looks down
in the room, where you lay,
He has already decided
if you will have another day.

The Intensive Care Unit,
a very intimate place to view,
a sacred place where God says
"I See You"

I have seen you love.
I have seen you hate.
I have seen you be impatient.
I have seen you wait.

I have seen you when you have given.
I have seen you when you take.
I have seen you when you sleep.
I have seen you when you wake.

I have seen you help others,
when no one else was around.
I have seen you pass the Homeless,
as they lay hungry on the ground.

I have seen you judge others,
when your own house was not clean.
I have seen you be compassionate,
instead of plain ole' mean.
I have seen you honor me with tithes,
when your circumstances were great.
I have seen you put your trust in me,
but then immediately
lose your faith.

As you lay there on a
cold and clammy
surface,
I already know if you still
indeed have purpose.

So as the bright light approaches
and you feel the need to move ahead,
God has already made the decision
"It is not your time to be physically dead!"

The bright light will grow dim as your
family calls you back.
Your heartbeat will resume beating,
while your blood flow stays on track.

You will hear familiar voices
in the background,
as doctors exhaust their skills,
but the final outcome of everything
will be based solely on God's will.

Oh what an intimate moment
Between God and you.
That sacred, scary and helpless place
that man calls
"I.C.U."

From God
Through Theresa
8/15/2010 - 3:52 p.m.

Citizens of Heaven

Before the foundations of the world
God already knew you by name.
From the midst of the firmament
The Holy Heaven was made.

While the earth was in the middle
and the seas were the firmament below,
The earth was dark, but the lights from
Heaven made it show.

Now the Heavens had a host of angels
But Lucifer was one of God's best.
He was the Archangel of Music,
until he began his self-seeking quest.

So God cast him out of the Heavens
and sent him to the earth.
He no longer held his title,
he was stripped of all his worth.

So disguised as a serpent
He slithered on the ground.
Looking to start confusion
until Adam and Eve
He found.

Lucifer said unto the woman
"Eat this fruit you were forbidden
And ye shall not surely die."
What a big mistake they made,
they fell into his lie.

So now instead of eternal life,
Dust you were made and dust you shall return.
You will work until your dying day;
everything you have
you will earn.

Now man walks on earth with sin
and good choices he must make.
But when he chooses to do wrong,
altar sacrifices to God
he now must take.
Then God decided to
send Himself down
in the flesh,
He loved His creation so dearly,
He had to fix our mess.

So this part of Him He called
His Son
and Jesus was His name.
He walked the earth for many years
No sin on Him
could be blamed.

When His work was done and
God's Glory was redeemed
God decided to call Him back.

But in order to wash away
all of our sins
He had to withstand
a brutal attack.

His bloodshed was the sacrifice,
so that we could commune with God.
Our sins will now be forgiven
Eternal life is no longer a facade.

So now that everything is in place,
This is when the true battle on earth starts.
Will you follow Satan or worship Jesus
with all your heart?

This will be when the call begins
To see who you will serve.
For everyone will receive this call,
but only a few will have the nerve.

If you are the chosen one that answers the call
during your internal fight,
you will become a "Citizen of Heaven"
On earth you must be the light.

Where there is darkness,
is where you should be,
With the help of The Comforter,
You will set the sinners free.

Before the foundations of the earth,
God already knew you by name.
From the midst of the firmament
"Citizens of the Heavens"
were already made.

From God
Through Theresa
8/20/2010 - 5:33 a.m.

Armor of God

Put on the Helmet of Salvation
for it is yours to claim each and every day.
It is a covering over your mind
Because if left idle
becomes a place for the Devil to play.

Put on the Belt of Truth
for the truth will set you free.
It will allow you to see who you really are
but you must have a sincere relationship with thee.

"For I am the way, Truth and the Life.
No one comes to the Father except through me."
(John14:6)

Put on the Breast Plate of Righteousness
for the whole wide world to see.
Because of Jesus, you have been justified
and are now seen holy in the eyes
of the Almighty.

Put on your Sandals of Peace
and stand firm where ever you go,
spread the Good News that Jesus Christ is Lord
and the world's salvation shall surely grow.

Put on the Shield of Faith
and crucify yourself with Christ.
Live by the faith of the Son of God
His death was the ultimate sacrifice.

Put on the Sword of the Spirit
for it is the mighty power of God's Word.
It will cut through soul and spirit.
The victory is always ours, once it is heard.

So put on the Armor of God each and every day
before your feet touch the ground.
So that when the arrows and weapons of the
wicked world make their approach,
your blessings and protection will still abound.

From God
Through Theresa
11/6/2010 - 12:54 p.m.

The Land of No Return

I have taken the Lord Jesus as my salvation
and have said goodbye to my flesh
I am now renewed in the Spirit
and have committed to
life's biggest test

The Land of No Return

While drowning in a sea of darkness
a ray of light came into my view
I finally realized I could not do it my way
my total surrender
had to be given to You

I had to say good-bye to a lot of things,
some things were easier said than easier to do
but I knew that if I really wanted change
in my life I finally had to see these things through

I had let go of my "So Called" friends,
who were never my real friends at all
I had to stop following and start leading
I had to respond to God's Sovereign call

I could no longer go to the night clubs
and pretend that I just loved to dance
when honestly and truly
I was in search of true romance

I could no longer go to the liquor store
and buy a pint of Rum to drink
when really I was drinking
so that I wouldn't have to think

I could no longer hold bitterness
towards people, who betrayed me and treated me mean
now I have to forgive them and
wash their slates completely clean

I could no longer sleep in on Sundays
because that day is now given to You
The other six days can be for me
so one day is the least I can do for You

I could no longer take my entire check
and give nothing to You at all
now I must give You at least ten percent
so that generational curses
will not befall

I could no longer open my mouth in anger
and let profanities take control
now that I am a child of God
this type of language convicts my soul

While drowning in a sea of darkness
a ray of light came into my view
I finally realized I could not do it my way
my total surrender
had to be given to You

I had to say good-bye to a lot of things
some things were easier said than easier to do
but I knew that if I really wanted change
in my life
I finally had to see these things through

The Land of No Return

From God
Through Theresa
11/6/2010 - 9:45 p.m.

The Puppet

I have been renewed in the spirit
and my fleshly ways have become dead
I no longer control the thoughts in my head

I now belong to Jesus

I am now accepted by God

My thoughts are no longer my thoughts
and my ways are no longer my ways
I am now on a string that is guided
by God
He tells me what to do and say
each and every day

When I wake, I remove my flesh
and surrender myself to Him
My body is now
His temple
I must allow the Holy Spirit
to control each and every limb

I am now a Puppet for Jesus

If the Spirit says to love
when my flesh tells me to hate
Because I belong to him,
this is now a short debate

If my Spirit says to help
when my flesh says to ignore
I will now become convicted inside
because Jesus is behind the door!

I am now a Puppet for Jesus

If my Spirit says to wait
when my flesh tells me to go
I must now sit and wait patiently
for there will be something
He's trying to show

If my Spirit says to give
when my flesh wants to keep
I will now give no matter what
for more abundant blessings
I will surely reap

I am now a Puppet for Jesus

If the Spirit wants to heal
when the flesh says just sit back
Now you will lay hands on the sick
No matter if Satan attacks

I am now a Puppet for Jesus

Invisible strings being pulled by God's angels above
destroying your flesh daily and giving you
loving righteous tugs
helping you to make the right decisions to do things
you normally would not do
removing your feelings completely
and doing what Jesus would do

I am now a Puppet for Jesus

I am now accepted by God

From God
Through Theresa
11/26/2010 - 10:49 p.m.

Obedience

What could be better than gifts and jewels?
Who is smarter the wise man or the fool?
If you are good, are you better than
someone who is bad?

God, the Creator and the Maker of all things
What type of sacrifice do you give such a King?

If you sacrifice your time on Sunday
will that be enough?
While working the other six days
this sacrifice seems very tough.

If you put something in the church bucket,
even though it is not your tithes,
will He understand?
Will it be enough to stop the curse placed
upon your families lives?

If you truly love your parents,
but do not respect what they tell you to do
Will you live a shorter life or will your years on earth
continue to accrue?

If you steal because you are hungry
because the fear of starving has gripped your soul
and what little faith you had
in God providing, has
vanished and now struggling has taken its toll

Will He understand
and adjust His commandment for you?

If you fornicate
but you are truly in love
and you are just waiting
for it to be the right time for you,
Will He understand even if it is not blessed by Him
and marriage is no longer in view?

If you have a lot of money
and give generously to the poor,
should that excuse the way you live in the world,
even if it is a life He deplores?

Even though Adam and Eve ate off the forbidden tree,
and God's orders they chose to ignore
Do you think their goodness should have been considered
before He closed the eternal door?

Your Obedience is Greater than your Sacrifices!
He does not want your jewels, silver or your gold
He desires for you to simply do what you are told!

For He is the Creator and the Maker of all things
So your sacrifices are His already
Your Tithes are His
Your Jewels are His
Your Gold is His
Your Time is His
Your Money is His
Your Goat is His
Your Calf is His
Your Offerings are His
Your Food is His
Your Fasting is His
Your Goodness is His
Your Body is His
Your Spirit is His
Your Sundays are His
Your Children are His
Your Parents are His
Your Home is His
Your Job is His
Your Love is His
Your Peace is His
Your Joy is His
Your Kindness is His
Your Self Control is His
Your Gentleness is His
Your Patience is His
Your Death is His
Your Life is His

God, the Creator and the Maker of all things
What type of sacrifice do you give such a King?
The type of sacrifice you give such a King;
The Owner, Creator and Maker of all things

OBEDIENCE

Now therefore, if ye will obey my voice indeed,
and keep my covenant,
then ye shall be a particular treasure unto me above all people,
for all the earth is mine. (Exodus 19:5)

Thank God, for Jesus
for with His blameless obedience and bloodshed,
You are able to Receive
The greatest sacrifice ever made
by such a King
because
Jesus was already His

From God
Through Theresa
12/22/2010 - 9:54 a.m.

Glory

The supernatural manifestation of His presence
The all-consuming fire on the mountain top
The painful and wonderful transformation
of all things He beholds
as He refines and purifies its remains.

Remove the veil from your heart and see who you really are.
Father of ubiquity and great holiness
The most brilliant light of goodness
Causing the eternal heavens
to replace the need of the sun and the moon
While illuminating the lamb
to receive His glory.

Honor, praise and distinction, are His
for the manifestation of all creation.
Through His mighty actions,
majestic are His deeds and His righteousness
endures forever.

Remove the veil from your heart and see who you really are.
He's above and beyond all human comprehension
A mighty pillar of clouds and fire,
provider of darkness and light.
Creating our protection and guidance
through the night.

Oh Shekinah!
How blessed I would be
to have
His goodness pass by me.
This powerful thing seen in man and in the earth
but it is not of them, but for Him.
Like a rainbow in a cloud on a rainy day
Oh Gracious One
full of mercy, longsuffering
and abounding in goodness and truth
whose character reveals the highest form of love.

He who will exalt every valley
and will make every mountain and hill low
Every crooked place straight
and every rough place smooth
The One who goes across ahead of you
like a devouring fire.

Remove the veil from your heart and see who you really are.
King of kings and the Lord of lords
The Alpha and the Omega
The Beginning and the End
The Author and the Finisher of your Faith.

He is omniscient
"You know when I sit down and when I rise up;
You discern my thoughts from afar."
(Psalms 139:2)

He is omnipresent
"If I take the wings of the morning
and dwell in the most uttermost parts of the sea,
even there Your hand shall lead me,
and your right hand shall hold me."
(Psalms 139:9-10)

He is omnipotent
"I praise You, for I am fearfully and wonderfully made.
wonderful are Your works; my soul knows it very well."
(Psalms 139:14)

Remove the veil from your heart and see who you really are.
Oh mighty One who will call to the North
and call to the South
"Bring back my sons from far away and my daughters
from the ends of the earth!"
All called by His name and made for His glory.

The Heavens declare His Glory and the firmament shows his
handiworks
His law is perfect
His testimony sure
His precepts right
His commandments pure
With clean fear and true judgment
Altogether, both more desirable than gold.

Remove the veil from your heart and see who you really are.
He has mercy on whom He wishes to have mercy

and compassion on whom He wishes to have compassion.
Oh Gracious One
Slow to anger, abounding in love and faithfulness
Maintaining love to many
Forgiver of wickedness, rebellion and sin;
Yet He does not leave the guilty unpunished
Generations after generations, to the third and to the fourth
will answer.

Sustaining all things by His
powerful word, His Son is His glory.
His Glory shines like jasper and clear crystal
He is Holiness
Holy, Holy, Holy is Thy Name
Holiness is His totality.

Remove the veil from your heart and see who you really are.
Oh let us bow and kneel at his feet;
Worthy is the Lamb, who was slain,
to receive power and wealth and wisdom
and strength and honor and
Glory and praise!'
To him who sits on the throne and to the Lamb
be praise and honor and Glory
and power forever and ever.
Amen!
(Revelation 5.11-14)

From God
Through Theresa
1/27/2011 - 2:11 p.m.

If You Could See What I See

If you could see what I see
Oh how different your life would truly be...

For I see the greatness I have implanted in you,
The things you are able of achieving
You haven't got a clue.

Before the foundations of the earth,
I already knew you by name.
I counted every hair on your head
No two of you are the same.

You see when you were conceived
It was not by accident.
You were made with a purpose
You were made with My consent.

Through you, I would receive my glory
So I had to make some victories for you.
I have your blessings waiting to be poured out,
but first there are some things that you must do.

You must walk by faith and not by sight.
You must believe I will provide for you
even when things do not seem
to be going just right.

You must come outside of your comfort zone
and enter into unknown spaces.
You must be willing to walk out and seek the lost
in cruel and sometimes dangerous places.

If you could see what I see
Oh how different your life would truly be…

For you would do the impossible
because you would know that I am there.
You would take on life's greatest challenges
without a worry or a single care.

You would pay your tithes and offerings
and not question how it's spent.
You would love Me so much more
you would give more than ten percent.

You would feed the homeless
and be used to give healing to the sick.
You would call out Demons
No need for a weapon or stick.

You would tell alcohol
that it could not become your friend.
You would only ask for Me, the Savior,
in your time of need for I, you would only depend.

You would not condemn yourself
for yesterday's mistake.
You would instantly forgive yourself
My convictions you would rather take.

If you could see what I see
Oh how wonderful your life would truly be…

For your dreams would become your reality
because your faith would make them real.
They would no longer be just idol thoughts
mind images to keep concealed.

If you could see what I see
Oh how truly different this world would be…

For everyone would always being striving
to do their very best.
They would always be ready
to deal with any test.

They would reach for the moon
and catch the stars.
They would love one another
no matter how far.

They would feed the hungry
and provide help for the sick.
They would provide shelter for the homeless
and be prepared for Satan's tricks.

Oh if you could see what I see,
The world would be different indeed...

From God
Through Theresa
3/20/2011 - 6:18 p.m.

The Passover

The Blood of the Lamb
What a Holy Sacrifice
Bloodshed to wash away our sins
Sins that have no human price

Blood that was placed on our doors
So that the Angel of Death
would pass and leave
killing all of Egypt's firstborn
because they simply would not heave

What did God Pass Over for you?
Because Jesus paid the cost
What are you still causing
God's heart to grieve about
While knowing His Son's blood was shed
and His flesh was nailed to the Cross

If you have accepted his Son as your
Savior
what did He Save you from?
You fought and fought and fought and fought
What made you finally succumb?

Were you tired of doing it your way?
When your way was always wrong
Were you tired of acting like things were fine?
When really inside you were weak and not
Strong!

Then one night when your world became black
And no one else was there to be found
Did you fall to your knees and cry out to God?
Did you painfully hit the ground?

Ah! Is that when you decided to confess your sins
And take the Lord Jesus as your Savior?
Is that when God's Son's sacrifice
Began to work in your humble favor?

What did God Pass Over for you?
What sins of yours have been washed clean?
Washed clean, so that your presence in front of
The Almighty God would be seen

Has He passed over your hatred?
Has He passed over your lies?
Has He passed over your lack of kindness?
When you should have been chastised

Has He passed over your jealousy?
Has He passed over your affair?
Has He passed over your drinking?
When you really didn't care

Has He passed over your laziness?
Has He passed over your addictions?
Has He passed over your fornication?
Thank God for His convictions!

Has He passed over your murder?
Has He passed over your rape?
Has He passed over the things in your life
that man would not allow you to escape?

What did God Pass Over for you?
Because His precious Son's Blood was shed?
What sins of yours have been taken away
So that you would have life
and not be dead?

You can now go beyond the gate
and boldly face your God
The Blood of the Lamb
The most Holy Sacrifice
deserves a sovereign nod

From God
Through Theresa
4/6/2011 - 10:50 p.m.

Hurt People Hurt People

Tooth for a Tooth and an Eye for an Eye
Didn't you know, that was just a lie.
Two wrongs do not make a right
Even when you are hurting
The answer is not to fight.

Hurt People, Hurt People

A life full of disappointments,
people always letting you down,
When you needed help in your darkest time
no family or friends were around.

Hurt People, Hurt People

Relationship after relationship
You feel like you gave all you had.
Looking for love in all the wrong places
Because you had no Mom or Dad.

Hurt People, Hurt People

Getting in and out of trouble
Hanging around with the wrong friends,
Looking for someone's attention
feeling neglected from within.

Hurt People, Hurt People

Watching your little brother
have no shoes to wear,
And then at dinner time
you hear
there is hardly any food to spare.

Hurt People, Hurt People

You were just a little child
when your mother and dad would fight,
Feeling scared and helpless
unable to sleep throughout the night.

Hurt People, Hurt People

Being bullied at school each day
for no apparent reason,
Harboring all of you anger and tears
through every single season.

Hurt People, Hurt People

Losing some of your best friends
because of the color of your skin,
Forced to forget and overlook
your great qualities from within.

Hurt People, Hurt People

Cheated on and sexually abused,
Emotionally damaged and physically bruised
No longer wanting to be spiritually used.

Hurt People, Hurt People

A world full of Hurt with no joy to be found
Destroys the entire spirit man
The soul is slowly drowned.

Hurt People, Hurt People

Then a wall is built to protect your heart
and you only let a few people in,
Being nice becomes impossible
and hurting others a personal win.

But if you allow God to
restore and to heal
all of the hurt and pain that you have been through
Many more victories, you will see
Your mind will be renewed.

Hurt People, Heal

From God
Through Theresa
6/5/2011 4:17 a.m.

The Majority

It does not matter what challenges
you are in
It does not matter if there are
twenty to defend

If you and God stand side by side
You and Him equal the Majority
and the Majority
will always win!

A room full of people
could disagree with your point of view
But it will not matter to stand all alone
Only God needs to be in agreement with you!

You and Him equal the Majority
And the Majority
Will always win!

You might look at a situation
and it will seem too much for you
to bear
But if God says you can handle it,
then you know
He must be near

You and Him equal the Majority
and the Majority
will always win!

Right is right
and wrong is wrong
and the truth shall always set you
free
As long as God is on your side
you are destined for victory

Greater is He who is in me
then he who is in the world
(1 John 4:4)

You and He equal the Majority
and the Majority
will always win!

From God
Through Theresa
6/5/2011 - 7:58 p.m.

God Encounter

Every day before your feet hit the floor
You should surrender yourself
to the Almighty God
He will already have a
daily mission for you
So you can receive His sovereign nod

Who knows what that mission will be
It could be as simple as a hug or a smile
But no matter what He assigns you to do
I can assure you it will be worthwhile

You should always be
a God Encounter

He might ask you to feed the homeless
He might ask you to assist one in distress
But no matter what your assignment is for the day
It is important to fulfill His requests

You should always be a
God Encounter

He might ask you to speak to someone
who's rude and cruel
or even work with a simple fool
But no matter what your assignment
is for the day

You should always be a
God Encounter

He might ask you to help the sick
or even give wise and encouraging words
to women who do daily tricks
But no matter what your assignment
is for the day

You should always be a
God Encounter

No matter where you go
No matter what you do
The world should
always see the God in you!

You should always be a
God Encounter!

From God
Through Theresa
6/5/2011 - 11:32 p.m.

Panners

Faults, mistakes, trash,
and baggage
We all have some of this
But if you are looking for my golden part
you must take time to sift

If you take the time to
Shake me left and then shake me right
My dirt will come apart
And the only thing that will be left to see
Will be what has remained
Within my heart

Without a heart you would not live
So it definitely has a need
And even though it may be cluttered with
Junk
Beneath the mess - it surely breathes

Panning for character is like panning for
Gold
The dirt always shows up first
But then after shaking
you realize
the good will come to surface
and the bad must slowly submerse

Panning for someone's goodness
is always easier to say
than to do
for it takes time and patience to find
It takes time to be
brought into view

God is looking for the earth's Panners
The one's willing to shake through someone else's dirt
God is looking for Panners
The one's willing to dig through the hurt

Faults, mistakes, trash,
and baggage
We all have some of this
But if you are looking for the Golden part
you must take time to sift

From God
Through Theresa
6/18/2011 - 9:30 p.m.

www.ingramcontent.com/pod-product-compliance
Lightning Source LLC
Chambersburg PA
CBHW050555300426
44112CB00013B/1922